Just Tasting

Quick and Easy Recipes
mini appetizers, soups & salads
for casual entertaining

by Robert Zollweg

Designed and written by Robert Zollweg
Photography by Rick Luettke, www.luettkestudio.com
Graphics by Gary Raschke and Robert Zollweg
Art Direction by Gary Raschke

Library of Congress Cataloging-in-Publication Data:

Just Tasting
Mini Appetizers, Soups and Salad Recipes
for Casual Entertaining by Robert Zollweg

ISBN 978-1-4507-5825-3

Printed in the United States of America
By: R. R. Donnelley and Company

I'd like to dedicate this cookbook to the one person who many years ago taught me a few simple rules about entertaining and the art of presentation.

Aunt Peg Zollweg (1911-2004)

There are so many people to thank for making this cookbook a reality.

My mother, Virginia, my kids, Christopher and Rhonda,
Steve Tester, Elaine Bender, Richard and Sandy,
Lori Luscombe, Mona Shousher.

Linda Traxler, my big sis, we miss her

No one was there more for me than Gary Raschke.
He knows more about computer technology than I will ever know.
His graphic and art direction skills are insurmountable,
I owe him so much and I thank him.

Lots of others I want to mention;
Fran Breitner, Rosie Jordan, Beth Baroncini, Karen Barentzen,
Vicki Richardson, Gina Baccari, Cathie Logan, Tom Fratantuono,
Denise Grigg, Kelly Kelley, Roger Williams, Jeff Joyce, Serena Williams,
Amy Lewarchik, Greg Pax, Brooks Clayton, Natalie Brunner, Tom Kull,
Mary Jo Conn, Sandy Shultz, Brionna Richmond, Melissa Fleig.

Carlos, Cindy and David
Nancy, Michael, Claudia, Nicole and Lisa

But most of all, Brenda Bennett and Libbey Glass
for giving me the opportunity to do what I enjoy doing.

Table of Contents

Introduction 8 - 9

Containers, Preparation and Serving 10 - 15

Quick and Easy Appetizers 16 - 39

Cold Appetizers 40 - 47

Hot Appetizers 48 - 73

Hearty Soups 74 - 85

Bisques and Cream Soups 86 - 99

Cold or Chilled Soups 100 - 107

Mini Salads 108 - 123

Index 124 - 125

Introduction

Just Tasting is a trendy way to say "you are invited over for a sampling of wonderful little appetizers, soups and salads that will be presented on little plates and in little bowls." I've adapted many of my favorite recipes to fit into these little containers just because they look so darn cute. They make for a fabulous presentation and by the way, they taste great and are easy as can be to prepare. All the ingredients can be found in any local grocery store.

Just Tasting is also about presentation. Any one of these recipes can be made by itself, but a group of them together is what tasting is all about. Little bits of this and that, presented together beautifully is what will bring it all together.

I first heard about all these mini servings of appetizers, soups, salads and even desserts at the National Restaurant Show in Chicago a couple of years ago. Restaurants were seeing an increase in popularity with serving appetizers and soups in small containers. As a result, they started developing and serving these items in petite or taster versions. To make them special and more exciting, they found small glass and ceramic containers to show off their new creations. As a result, mini tasters have taken the foodservice industry by storm. They are usually served in multiples with a variety of different mini appetizers or soups to choose from, similar to Spanish tapas. I felt this was something today's consumers would love and were missing in the marketplace, especially when it came to home entertaining. Most of the following mini taster recipes are pretty quick and simple to make. Some do take a little longer, but none will take longer than 30 minutes to complete, which is important with today's lifestyles in home entertaining. Most of us don't have the time or patience to spend hours in the kitchen preparing and cleaning up from a complicated recipe. So I've created this little collection of recipes that will hopefully, make your next cocktail party a huge success.

Mini soups tasters are usually served in various 2 to 3 ounce containers and in multiples. This is so all your guests can try a small sampling of a few different soups.

Mini appetizers are always cut and served in small bite size pieces. These are especially interesting when served on a rectangular server or on small appetizer plates. Visit your local retailer and select a series of small bowls and plates.

Displaying mini appetizers and soups is key to a festive party or get together. Using a variety of different servers and tiered trays helps with this fashionable and trendy presentation. See photos on the following pages for a few creative ideas. These presentations are great for special parties and birthdays, to name a few. You will look very professional and your guests will love you.

I hope you enjoy these wonderful little mini appetizer and soup recipes as much as I have in creating them. I have been using them for years. They are quick and simple and most are just fun to make. Making a variety of appetizers for a tasting party is just so much fun and very rewarding. Add some unusual beverages to the mix. A festive party punch served in really cool tall glasses or wine in little cordial glasses.

Working in the tabletop industry has been so very rewarding and it is where I have learned so much about entertaining. I love to entertain and I hope that Just Tasting with its mini appetizers and soups will be a great way for you to turn your next festive occasion or cocktail party into something really special.

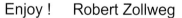

Enjoy !   Robert Zollweg

Containers

Preparation

Serving Suggestions

The following pages will show you a few easy steps in the preparation of the mini tasting recipes, short cuts when time is so important and some tips on presentation to make this tasting party a fun and festive occasion for you and your guests.

Remember the golden rule, always make your guests feel at home. Always have food and beverages that are common to your guests tastes. Sometimes you can go just a little beyond to experiment, but not too far. They need to feel comfortable and you need to be relaxed and at ease for your enjoyment, too. Parties should not be stressful, so keep it simple and casual. These recipes, along with your favorite beverages will help guarantee a successful tasting party. Enjoy !

Containers

Below are some of the containers I will use to show off these delicious tasting recipes. There are so many wonderful containers that can be used to serve any of these tasting recipes. Use your imagination. Tall shooter glasses make a wonderful container for cold soups and gelatin salads. Small ceramic ramekins and shot glasses work great for hot soups. Small mini bowls, platters or plates are great for tasting appetizers.

Many of your favorite recipes can be made into mini tasters. If you cannot prepare them in small dishes, you can always serve them in small dishes.

Be creative, there are many choices of mini taster containers to choose from. The containers I used in this publication can be purchased from various area retailers.

Preparation

All you need to get started on creating these great tasting recipes are some ordinary kitchen tools: a mixing bowl, measuring cups, spoons, spatulas and a kitchen funnel. A blender or food processor is also helpful. There are a number of different tools in the marketplace for making it easier to fill these small tasting dishes. Pictured above is a commercial decorating press and filling tool for creating beautiful cheese spread decorations on crackers or toast and filling small containers with a creative flare. You can also use a simple kitchen funnel, pastry bag or even a one quart storage bag with the corner cut off for filling smaller containers. All can be purchased at your area retailers. They are very helpful in filling the smaller items for a very professional touch. I love to use them. They are simple to operate and very easy to clean.

Using a standard kitchen funnel to fill smaller containers is one tool you cannot live without in the kitchen when making mini tasters. I usually pour my hot soup into a measuring cup with a nice pour lip when filling small bowls or dishes. It makes it so easy to fill any container with a small opening. I will even use a funnel when I am filling the small ceramic bowls with a hot bisque or cream soup. It keeps the side walls clean and neat looking. Individual servings of soup in little ceramic or glass containers is what "Just Tasting" is all about.

Serving Presentations

When I'm entertaining at home, I use a variety of mini appetizers on different platters and servers. They can be made of glass, ceramic or stainless steel. Use your favorite beverages to compliment your mini tasters. Always remember to compliment your appetizers, something plain, something spicy, unless you are having a theme party, where you want only Mexican or Italian foods. Otherwise, try mixing up the selection so that all your guests will have something different to try and enjoy.

This soup trio is a new trendy way to serve 3 different tasting soups to your guests as an appetizer before dinner.

Here is a fun idea. Try using this mini brandy glass to serve chilled soup or try using a martini glass for desserts or a cordial stem for a jello salad. These are a few ideas on how to use different products in your home to serve these great tasting recipies.

Here's an example of a mini soup and salad buffet with various tasting recipes. This would be a great buffet for your guests right before they leave for a movie or concert, something light and festive. This will take just a little extra effort, but you will receive rave reviews.

Quick and Easy Appetizers

Italian Bruschetta

This is about as Italian as it gets. Chunky tomatoes and pesto served on crispy garlic toast. You can make it on any shape or kind of toast. I like a French baguette, sliced diagonally. You will need a long, narrow platter for serving, see photo at right.

1 - 24" loaf of hard-crusted French baguette, thinly sliced and toasted dark.
1/2 stick of butter or margarine
garlic salt
5-6 ripe tomatoes, diced
1/2 cup pesto sauce
1 Vidalia onion, finely chopped
1/4 cup finely chopped fresh cilantro or parsley
blacks olives, optional

Slice the French bread into 1/2" diagonal slices. Spread a little butter on each piece of bread. Sprinkle with a little garlic salt. Toast in broiler until brown. Remove from broiler and let cool slightly. Spread each piece of toast with some pesto sauce.

Combine the tomatoes, chopped onions, parsley and olive oil together until well blended. Place about one rounded tablespoon of mixture on a slice of toasted bread and spread evenly. Arrange the bruschetta on a long, narrow platter. Serve and Enjoy !

Italian Bruschetta with Cheese Spread

You will need 8 oz cream cheese, softened and 2-3 finely chopped green onions. Combine and mix well. Spread about one heaping teaspoon of cheese mixture on toasted bread. Add the tomato mixture from above. Arrange on long platter and serve. Enjoy !

Beef and Pickle Roll Ups

It doesn't get any easier than this. These are quick, easy and very tasty. I borrowed this tasty recipe from the Bender Family. You will need a long narrow platter for serving or several small square appetizer plates, see photo at right.

1/2 lb dried beef or deli baked ham
1 jar of deli dill pickles, sliced in long thin slices
4 oz cream cheese
handful of toothpicks

Take a piece of dried beef or ham, spread about a teaspoon of cream cheese over the beef or ham. Then add a slice of dill pickle. Roll it up to form a tube. You can cut it in half if you want smaller pieces. The cream cheese will hold it together or use a toothpick. Arrange on a platter or small plates and serve. Enjoy !

Salami and Cheese Roll Ups

This is another simple and easy appetizer, but a real party pleaser. You will need a square server or a long narrow platter for serving. See photo at right.

1 lb salami or baked deli ham, thinly sliced
1 lb baby swiss cheese or cheddar cheese
handful of toothpicks
1/4 cup spicy mustard

Take a piece of salami or ham, place a piece of cheese of top, spread a little spicy mustard on top and roll up. Use a toothpick to hold it together. Arrange on a unique serving platter or individual tasting plates. Enjoy !

Prosciutto and Melon

This is another traditional Italian appetizer, but here it is made as finger food appetizer. These are great by the platterful. You will need a long narrow platter for serving or some small appetizer plates, see photo at right.

handful of toothpicks
one ripe cantaloupe melon
1/2 lb prosciutto or ham, thinly sliced
freshly ground black pepper
a little olive oil

You can substitute papaya, mango or pear for the melon or try a combination of all.

If using a melon, cut it in half, remove the seeds, cut into 1" slices and remove the rind. Cut the slices into bite size chunks.

Cut the prosciutto or ham in 1" wide long strips.

Take a chunk of melon, wrap it in the piece of prosciutto, hold it together with a toothpick. Drizzle each piece with a little olive oil and a sprinkle of fresh pepper. Arrange on a unique serving platter or small appetizer plates and serve. Enjoy !

Feta Cheese Toast

A delicious, light and snappy cheese spread that will please everyone. You will need a long narrow platter for serving, see photo at right.

1 loaf of hard crusted French baguette, thinly sliced and toasted. You can also use regular sliced Italian bread or any plain cracker.

8 oz crumbled feta cheese
8 oz cream cheese, softened
1 green onion, finely chopped
2 tbsp dried parsley flakes

handful of sliced black or green olives, optional

For an added twist, try adding some chopped pimentos or pecans to the cheese mixture.

Combine the first 3 ingredients until well blended. Place about one tablespoon of mixture on a slice of toasted bread and spread evenly. Garnish wlth 2-3 pieces of sliced olives in the center. Sprinkle with parsley flakes. Arrange on a long narrow platter or any fancy platter and serve. Enjoy !

Mozzarella, Tomato & Basil Caprese

You have to love all these Italian appetizers. Here is another one that is just fabulous and equally delicious. It goes great with the Prosciutto and Melon (page 22) and Italian Bruschetta (page 18). This is a great appetizer anytime of year because cherry tomatoes are readily available. It is very refreshing, colorful and simple to make.

You will need at least 20 long cocktail toothpicks and a beautiful long serving tray or several small appetizer plates, see photo at right.

20 mini buffalo mozzarella balls, about 3/4" diameter
40 cherry tomatoes
bunch of fresh basil
fresh ground pepper and some Italian spices
20 large pitted black olives, optional

any kind of Italian or balsamic vinaigrette dressing

If you can't find the mini mozzarella balls, use a large chunk of fresh mozzarella, cut into bite size pieces.

Take a cocktail toothpick and start with a cherry tomato, basil, a mozzarella ball, more basil, then a tomato, and if you want, more basil and end with a black olive. It is so easy and they look great on a serving tray or in a glass bowl. Drizzle with Italian vinaigrette dressing and sprinkle with some spices. Serve and Enjoy !

For traditional serving of Caprese, start with a slice of fresh tomato on a small appetizer plate. Add a slice of fresh mozzarella cheese, some fresh basil, drizzle some balsamic vinegar and top with fresh ground pepper and some Italian spices. I sometimes add chopped black olives. See photo at right. Enjoy !

Festive Olive Kabobs

This one is so simple and easy, but your guests will just gobble them up. Here is another one to use with the other Italian appetizers.

You will need about 24 long cocktail toothpicks and a serving tray or small glass bowl, see photo at right.

jar of large pimento stuffed green olives
a can of large pitted black olives
large chunk of swiss, provolone or mozzarella cheese, cubed

You can use only green or black olives if that is what you like. Sometimes I put all black on some and all green on the others. Jazz it up with some specialty olives from your local grocery store deli department.

Take a cocktail toothpick and start with a green olive, then black, then green and finally a black olive. Add a chunk of cheese between the olives. It's that simple. Stack them on a long serving tray or in a bowl and you are ready to go. Serve and Enjoy !

Bacon Spread on Toast

This makes a great dip or spread if you don't want to make appetizers out of it. I love it either way. You will need a unique serving platter, see photo at right.

1 loaf of hard-crusted French baguette, thinly sliced and toasted dark. You can also use any plain cracker.

4 oz crumbled feta or blue cheese, more or less, depending on your taste
8 oz cream cheese, softened
5-6 slices of crispy bacon, crumbled
one stalk of finely chopped celery
1 green onion, finely chopped
dried or fresh parsley for garnish

Make sure the cheeses are room temperature and softened. Combine all the ingredients until well blended. Leave a strip of bacon for garnishing on top. Place about one tablespoon of mixture on a slice of toasted bread and spread evenly. Sprinkle with a little crumbled bacon and dried parsley. Arrange on a long narrow platter and serve. Enjoy !

Deviled Egg Spread on Toast

This egg spread can also be made into little tea sandwiches. Either way, they are delicious. You will need a long narrow platter or several tasting plates for serving, see photo at right.

1 loaf of hard-crusted French baguette (2" to 3" round), thinly sliced and toasted dark. You can also use any whole grain bread cut into strips and toasted. I sometimes just use plain crackers or melba toast.

6 hard boiled eggs, shelled and chopped
3 tbsp sour cream
1-1/2 tbsp mayonnaise
1 tsp spicy mustard
1/2 tsp lemon juice
salt and coarse black pepper to taste
handful of sliced green or black olives for garnish (optional)
some finely chopped parsley or thyme for garnish

For a unique twist, try adding crumbled bacon, chopped green onions, fresh tarragon or chopped green chilies.

Combine the first six ingredients until well blended. The more coarse you leave the mixture the better. Place about one tablespoon of mixture on a slice of toasted bread and spread around. Sprinkle with a little parsley or thyme. Place 2-3 sliced olives down the center of the toast. Arrange on a long narrow platter or on small individual tasting plates and serve. Enjoy !

Ham and Pineapple on Skewers

Simple and delicious, you will need about 30 long cocktail toothpicks, see photo at right.

5-6 slices of cooked ham, cut 1/2" thick, and then into 1" cubes
1 large can of pineapple, drained but save some juice
1/2 cup dark brown sugar
one jar of maraschino cherries, optional

Take a long toothpick, place a piece of ham, piece of pineapple and then a cherry.
Repeat until all the skewers are filled. It's that simple.

In a mixing bowl, combine the pineapple juice and brown sugar. Mix well. You may need to add a little more brown sugar to get the right consistency. Dip each of the skewers into the sauce until well coated.

Arrange on a long platter or several small appetizer plates. This can be served hot or cold.

Serve and Enjoy !

Simply Chutney

This is a very simple and delicious recipe. A quick appetizer that can be put together in minutes when you need something special when friends or family drop in before a special occasion. I usually serve these on a long narrow platter or a small square ceramic platter, see photo at right.

One box of any type cracker, like Triscuit, Ritz, or Carr's Crackers, etc.
8 oz cream cheese, softened
1 jar of chutney sauce or apricot preserves

Chutney is a little spicier than regular fruit preserves.

Place large dollop or teaspoon full of cream cheese on the cracker, flatten slightly making a divot. Sometimes I take a chunk of cream cheese and roll it in a ball, then flatten it slightly with a divot. Cover with a spoonful of chutney or preserves. It is as simple as that and just as delicious. Arrange on a tray or platter and serve. Enjoy !

Cucumber Tea Sandwiches

These are so fun to make and are simply delicious in the summer when you need something light and refreshing to go along with a nice glass of Pinot Grigio. This recipe will make at least 20-25 little tea sandwiches. You will need a long, narrow white ceramic serving platter, see photo at right.

one loaf of party rye or any thin rye bread cut into 2" squares
8 oz cream cheese, softened
1/4 cup sour cream
1 tsp onion salt or 1/4 cup finely chopped green onions
1 cucumber, thinly sliced
1 tsp dill weed

I sometimes use a scalloped round or diamond shaped cookie cutter to make different shapes out of the rye bread, when I'm feeling more festive and have some extra time.

In a small bowl, mix together the softened cream cheese, sour cream and onion salt. Remove the crust from the rye bread and spread about a spoonful of cheese mixture on each piece of rye bread. Then a slice of cucumber. Sprinkle generously with dill weed and arrange on a platter and serve. Enjoy !

Cold Appetizers

Mango Salsa with Shrimp or Chicken

This is a wonderful addition to your appetizer buffet or cocktail party. For a more interesting presentation, serve this recipe in small individual square dishes or bowls, along with some small dessert spoons or cocktail forks, see photo at right.

1 lb of large frozen shrimp, rinsed and thawed
1 mango, peeled and finely cubed
12 oz fresh pineapple, diced
1/2 red pepper, finely chopped
1/2 green pepper, finely chopped
1/2 cup honey, divided in half
2 tsp red pepper flakes, optional

In a larger mixing bowl, combine the mango, pineapple and red and green peppers, half the honey and 1 tsp red pepper flakes, mix well. Place several spoonfuls of the mango salsa in each appetizer bowl.

In a small mixing bowl, place the rest of the honey and 1 tsp. red pepper flakes, dip the shrimp in the honey mixture. Place 2-3 shrimp in each individual appetizer bowl on top of the mango salsa.

This can be made in advance, but should be covered and refrigerated until ready to serve.

You can also use 2-3 boneless chicken breasts, cut into 3" long strips instead of the shrimp. The chicken should be grilled or pan fried until golden brown and done. Serve the same as the shrimp recipe from above.

Enjoy !

Sushi Teriyaki Clouds

This is another American version of Sushi. Serving it in little mini bowls just makes it even more unique and special. Place the little mini bowls on a large platter with a small bowl of teriyaki sauce in the center. See photo at right.

1 lb of smoked salmon or
2 boneless chicken breasts, grilled and cubed
few tablespoons of vegetable oil
one jar of teriyaki sauce
3 cups short grain rice, cooked as directed on the package
5 tbsp sugar
several green onions, finely chopped for garnish

Whether you are using smoked salmon or grilled chicken breasts, drizzle each piece with a little teriyaki sauce until coated. Break the smoked salmon into bite size pieces.

Prepare the rice as directed on the package but add the sugar to the water before adding the rice. Cook until all water is absorbed. Let stand for 15 minutes until cool.

In the small mini bowls, place a heaping spoonful of rice to fill the bowl. Make a small divot in the center. Fill the center with couple of pieces of either the chicken or salmon. Drizzle a little teriyaki sauce. Sprinkle with a few pieces of chopped green onion. Place the small bowls on a large platter and serve with a small bowl of teriyaki sauce. Enjoy !

Guacamole Roll Ups

This is not your conventional guacamole dip. You can add some spicy add-ons that make it unique for you and your guests. For a great presentation, use a long narrow rectangular serving platter with a side small bowl of spicy salsa. See photo at right.

handful of toothpicks
1 pkg corn or flour tortillas
1 large ripe avocado
2 tsp lemon juice
1/4 tsp salt
1 can green chilies, finely chopped
1 small onion, chopped
1 garlic clove, crushed
1 large ripe tomato, chopped
1 tsp crushed pepper
1 tsp worcestershire sauce

(if you are in a hurry, purchase guacamole from your local grocer)

You can add cooked ground beef or grilled chicken, chopped.

In a large mixing bowl, cut the avocado in half, peel and remove the pit. Use a fork to mash up the avocado coarsely. Mix in the remaining ingredients, gently as to keep it chunky.

Microwave the tortillas for a few seconds until warm. This will make them easier to handle. Place the tortillas on a flat surface, spread some of the guacamole mixture over half the tortillas shell. Add chopped chicken or ground beef. Roll it up. Cut into 2" pieces. Use a toothpick to hold together. Arrange on a long platter or individual mini bowls and serve with a small bowl of spicy salsa on the side. Serve and Enjoy !

Hot Appetizers

Stuffed Mushrooms

This is a great recipe to compliment any meat appetizer. When I'm in a real hurry, I'll use a boxed of stuffing mix. Sometimes I'll add some finely chopped chicken or beef to the stuffing. Preheat your oven to 350 degrees for the stuffed mushrooms. You will also need a large serving platter or several small appetizer plates, see photo at right.

24-30 medium-sized fresh mushrooms
1/2 cup bread crumbs or toasted rye or wheat bread, crumbled
1/2 cup sour cream
2 green onions finely chopped
1 stalk of celery, finely chopped

Rinse and dry the mushrooms thoroughly. Remove stems. Chop mushroom stems very fine. In a medium bowl, combine bread crumbs, sour cream, chopped mushroom stems, celery and green onions.

Place a small spoonful of stuffing mixture into the mushroom caps. Place stuffed mushrooms in a 9x13 baking dish, sprayed with a little non-stick cooking spray. Bake in a preheated oven at 375 degrees for 15 to 20 minutes until mushrooms are slightly tender. Arrange on a platter or in individual tasting bowls. These are great hot or at room temperature. Serve and Enjoy !

Cheese Cubes

If you like cheese, you will love this recipe. You can add different ingredients to make it a little spicy or a lot spicy. Try combining some different kinds of cheeses. You will need a large platter or several small tasting plates for serving, see photo at right. This will also make a great fondue dip.

1 large loaf of French bread, unsliced
1/2 cup butter
1 lb grated cheddar cheese
4 oz cream cheese
1 tsp worcestershire sauce
2 eggs, slightly beaten
2-3 green onions, finely chopped
1/4 cup finely chopped red bell pepper
1/4 tsp crushed red pepper, if you like spicy

You can also add some finely chopped chili peppers or bacon bits to the mixture.

Slice the French bread in thick 1" slices, remove crust. Cut into 1" cubes.

In a saucepan, stir butter and both cheeses over low heat until melted. Stir in worcestershire sauce, red bell pepper and chopped onions. Using a whisk, beat in eggs, whisk thoroughly. Add any additional ingredients now. Cook a few minutes longer.

Using a fork or tongs, dip each bread cube into the hot cheese mixture, turning to coat all sides. Place on a cookie sheet until cool. These can be served hot or at room temperature. Serve and Enjoy !

Chicken Teriyaki Kabobs

This recipe is one of my favorites. I love the tangy teriyaki sauce and the pineapple. This is also very good cooked on an outdoor grill. You will need at least 24 long cocktail toothpicks and a beautiful long serving tray or some small square appetizer bowls for individual servings, see photo at right.

4 fresh chicken breasts, cut into cubes
2 - 3 tbsp olive or vegetable oil
teriyaki sauce or sweet & sour sauce
1 can of pineapple chunks
1 large green pepper, cut into large pieces

Some lettuce and chopped red bell peppers for garnish, optional

You can purchase a jar of teriyaki sauce at your local grocer or use 1/2 cup dark brown sugar, 1/4 cup soy sauce, 1 tsp vinegar, 4 tbsp melted butter, mix together in a bowl.

In a large skillet, with a little oil, brown the chicken until done, add some teriyaki sauce and toss until coated. Remove from pan. Add a little more oil and some teriyaki sauce and saute the pineapple chunks and green pepper for about a minute, making sure all the pieces are well coated with teriyaki sauce. Do not overcook. Remove from pan.

Taking a large cocktail toothpick, start with a piece of pineapple, then the green pepper and then a piece of chicken. You can put them on the grill for a few minutes to brown them if you want. Cover the small appetizer plates or long serving platter with a layer of lettuce. Add the kabobs and sprinkle with finely chopped red bell pepper. Then drizzle any remaining teriyaki sauce over the kabobs. Serve and Enjoy !

Roasted Vegetable Tarts

This will make about 20 wonderful little Sicilian style pizzas or tarts. These are really delicious little tarts that are good hot or cold. You will need 2 cupcake or muffin pans and a large serving platter or several small tasting plates, see photo at right. Preheat oven to 425 degrees

2 pkg refrigerator rolls or biscuits
1 yellow and 1 green zucchini, cut into small pieces
2 red and yellow peppers, cut into small pieces
1 large sweet onion, coarsely chopped
2 oz parmesan cheese
1/2 cup cherry tomatoes, halved or 2 whole tomatoes, thinly sliced
3 tsp fresh thyme
salt & pepper
2 tbsp olive oil
1 tbsp balsamic vinegar (you can also use 1/4 cup of any balsamic salad dressing or Italian salad dressing)

Spray each of the muffin pans with non-stick cooking spray. Unroll the refrigerator rolls and separate. Cut each roll in half horizontally (to make a thin pastry roll). Place the thin pastry roll into the bottom of each of the muffin compartments. Press down.

In a large microwavable bowl, place all your cut up vegetables and microwave for a few minutes until the vegetables are slightly tender. Remove any liquid. Toss the vegetables with the olive oil and balsamic vinegar. Sprinkle with salt and pepper. Fill each of the muffin tins with a slice of tomato and some vegetable pieces. Sprinkle with parmesan cheese and a pinch of thyme.

Bake in the oven at 425 degrees for 10-12 minutes or until golden brown. Cool slightly and remove from pan. Can be served hot or at room temperature. Arrange on a beautiful oval platter or individual tasting plates and serve. Enjoy !

Hawaiian Sweet & Sour Meatballs

You will need a bunch of long cocktail toothpicks and a large narrow serving platter or several small mini appetizer plates, see photo at right.

1 lb of frozen 1" meatballs, thawed
1 large can of pineapple chunks, drain and save juice
2 green peppers, cut into 1" pieces
1/2 cup dark brown sugar
1/4 cup vinegar

In a baking pan, bake the meatballs at 350 degrees for about 30 minutes until browned. Remove from oven, drain any grease or liquid. In a microwavable bowl, microwave the green pepper pieces for a minute or so, until slightly tender.

Start with a toothpick, place a piece of pineapple, then green pepper and then a meatball. Repeat this until all your ingredients are depleted. You should end up with 20 - 25 kabobs.

In a small bowl, combine the pineapple juice, vinegar and brown sugar, stir until mixed thoroughly, adding a little more brown sugar if needed so the sauce is not too thick. Dip each skewer into the sauce or drizzle over the top of each. Place the skewers on a cookie sheet or baking pan. Keep warm in the oven at 200 degrees until ready to serve. Arrange on your serving trays and serve. Enjoy !

Mini Crab Cakes with Cucumber Dill Sauce

To make this a more exciting presentation, you will need about 12-15 little ceramic rectangular bowls or plates. You can also just arrange them on a long narrow or square platter, see photo at right.

2 tbsp fresh parsley, finely chopped
2 tbsp spicy mustard
1/2 tsp hot pepper sauce
1/4 tsp garlic powder
1 cup finely crushed crackers or bread crumbs
1 large egg, slightly beaten

1/4 cup mayonnaise
1 tsp worcestershire sauce
1/2 tsp salt
1 lb lump crabmeat
4 green onions, finely chopped

In a large bowl, mix all the ingredients except bread crumbs. Add about 10 tablespoons of crushed crackers or bread crumbs until everything is moistened. Shape the mixture into 1-1/2" balls and roll in the remaining crackers crumbs to coat. Flatten slightly.

Heat 3-4 tablespoons of oil in a large non-stick skillet over medium heat. Working in batches, fry the crab cakes until golden brown, about 3-4 minutes per side. You may need to add a little more oil with each batch. Transfer batches onto a cookie sheet and place in a warm oven until complete. Arrange crab cakes on the little tasting plates as pictured on the next page or on a larger platter.

To make the cucumber dill sauce, you will need 1/2 cup plain yogurt, 1/2 peeled cucumber chopped finely and mashed and 1 tsp dill weed. Mix together thoroughly.

Drizzle a little over each crab cake or place the sauce in a small bowl. Garnish with a slice of cucumber.

Serve and Enjoy !

Jambalaya Kabobs

This recipe puts a different twist on the traditional New Orleans recipe. I have served it on skewers to make appetizer kabobs, but you can serve it in individual little bowls for a delicious and unusual looking appetizer, see photo at right.

You will need about 25-30 long cocktail toothpicks or 15-20 little ceramic appetizer bowls.

3-4 boneless chicken breasts, cubed
3 tbsp vegetable oil
1 pkg precooked polish sausage, sliced into 1/2" slices
2 green peppers, cut into 1" squares
1 large sweet onion, cut into 1" squares
one package of frozen shrimp, thawed and rinsed
1-2 yellow or green zucchini, cubed
one large jar of spicy salsa or sweet & sour sauce

In a large skillet, add 3 tbsp vegetable oil and cubed chicken breasts. Saute until cooked and browned, about 10 minutes. Remove chicken. Add a little more oil and saute shrimp for one minute. Remove from pan. Add a little more oil and saute the vegetables for about 2 minutes or until slightly tender, but still firm, not soft. Keep all ingredients as hot as possible.

Take a long toothpick, place a piece of chicken, green pepper, onion, sausage, shrimp, onion and zucchini. Any combination will work. Place the salsa in a microwavable bowl and microwave until hot. Dip the kabobs in the salsa and arrange on a platter.

If you are serving the jambalaya in small bowls instead of as kabobs, toss all ingredients together in a large bowl with the salsa and divide equally into all the small tasting bowls.

Serve and Enjoy !

Pizza Mediterranean

I love to make these non-traditional flavored pizzas. You will need a large plain white ceramic platter or several small appetizer plates for serving. See photo at right.

Preheat oven to 425 degrees.

Buy one pizza crust from your local grocer if you want to make a traditional size pizza or you can make individual pizzas (my favorite way and very delicious) by using one package of regular refrigerator biscuits.

1 jar of artichoke hearts
5 oz fresh shredded mozzarella cheese
8 -10 fresh mushrooms, sliced
1/4 cup green onions, chopped
1/2 cup parmesan cheese
2 tbsp olive oil

When using biscuits, remove from tube, separate and cut in half horizontally. It should make about twenty 3" pizzas. On a cookie sheet, place the biscuits and flatten to about 3" in diameter. Brush the crusts with a little olive oil. If you like garlic flavor, add a little garlic salt to the olive oil or some crushed red pepper if you like things a little spicier

The mushrooms, mozzarella cheese and artichoke hearts should be chopped into smaller pieces when making the 3" pizzas. Leave them as larger chunks for a full size pizza.

Layer the artichoke hearts, mozzarella cheese, mushrooms, green onions on the pizza crust. Sprinkle each with a little parmesan cheese. Bake the larger pizza about 20 minutes and the smaller ones about 12-15 minutes until crispy brown. Arrange on a platter or individual appetizer plates and serve. Enjoy !

Meatballs with Spicy Sauce

These make a delicious and tasty little appetizer. For a quick version, buy frozen pre-cooked meatballs from your local grocer. You will need 12 -15 small appetizer plates, see photo at right.

4 cups fresh ground pork or beef, or combination
1 cup bread crumbs, from crusty bread
1 large onion, finely chopped
1 garlic glove, crushed
2 tbsp fresh parsley, finely chopped
1 egg, beatened
pinch of nutmeg, salt and pepper
flour for coating meatballs
2 tbsp olive oil
1 tsp lemon juice

Sauce
2 tbsp olive oil
1/2 cup chopped almonds
1/4 cup bread crumbs
1 garlic clove, crushed
2/3 cup white wine
1-1/2 cup beef broth
3 tbsp green onions, chopped

In a large mixing bowl, place the bread crumbs and sprinkle with enough water to moisten. Mix well. Add ground pork or beef, chopped onion, garlic, parsley. Mix thoroughly. Add beaten egg, nutmeg, salt and pepper. Mix well. Form mixture into small balls. Roll each of them in a little flour. In a large skillet, add a little oil and cook a few meatballs at a time for 4-5 minutes or so until brown. Work in batches.

To make the spicy sauce, heat 2 tbsp olive oil in the same skillet in which the meatballs were cooked. Add almonds, bread crumbs, saute a few minutes. Add garlic and green onions, cook a few more minutes. Add white wine, beef broth and the spices. Simmer a few more minutes.

Return the meatballs to the sauce in the skillet and cook on low heat for 30 minutes or so. Season with salt and pepper. Place 2-3 meatballs on each small plate and add a teaspoon of sauce over the meatballs. Serve and Enjoy !

Texas Party Quiches

This is one of my favorite recipes for a family brunch or get together. You will need 20 small 3 oz ramekins, suitable for baking. See photo at right.

Preheat oven to 350 degrees.

5 eggs, beaten
1/4 cup flour
1/4 cup butter or margarine, melted
1/4 cup of red bell pepper, finely chopped
1 can (4oz) chopped green chilies, drained
2 cups grated Monterey Jack cheese
1/4 cup cheddar cheese, optional
one jar of salsa for topping, optional

1 cup cottage cheese
1/2 tsp baking powder
4 tbsp finely chopped green onions
1 pkg refrigerator biscuits

You can add almost anything to this recipe, bacon, mushrooms, green pepper, etc.

Separate the biscuits and cut in half horizontally, making 20 pieces of thin pastry. I always spray my ramekins with a little non-stick cooking spray first. Place a piece of pastry into each ramekin, press down. Bake for 10 minutes at 350 degrees, until just brown and slightly puffy. You can make this quiche without the pastry crust.

In a large bowl, combine beaten eggs and cottage cheese. Beat in flour, baking powder and melted butter. Stir in Monterey Jack cheese, green onions, red bell pepper and chilies. Mix well. Pour mixture equally into the ramekins. Sprinkle a few pieces of cheddar cheese on top, optional. Bake in oven at 350 degrees for 20 minutes or until done. Serve warm, plain or with salsa on top or in a small side bowl.   Enjoy !

Egg Souffle

My family has been making this recipe for years. I have adapted it to these mini baking dishes which are great for family brunches or get togethers. You will need 15 -20 small 3 oz ramekins, suitable for baking. See photo at right.

Preheat oven to 350 degrees

6 eggs, beaten
1 cup milk
1 cup cheddar cheese, shredded
1 tsp mustard
1 lb cooked sausage, ham or ground beef
5-6 slices of coarse bread, lightly toasted and cubed

Sometimes I'll use croutons or stuffing mix on the bottom instead of crumbled bread.

You can add green pepper, mushrooms, green onions, chopped tomatoes, bacon, almost anything you would put in a western style omelet.

Put a layer of toasted bread cubes on the bottom of each of the ramekins or about 1/2 full. Add about a tablespoon of cooked sausage on top of bread cubes.

In a large bowl, combine beaten eggs, cheddar cheese, milk and mustard, mix thoroughly. Add any green onions, mushrooms, etc. to mixture now, mix well.

Pour mixture equally into the ramekins until full. Sprinkle a few pieces of cheddar cheese on top, optional. Bake in oven at 350 degrees for 20 minutes or until done. These will puff up very high and then flatten out once they are slightly cool. Serve warm.   Enjoy !

French Toast Souffle

This is another one of my favorites for a big family brunch. I will make this recipe along with the Texas Quiche or Egg Souffle. You will need 15 -20 small 3oz ramekins, suitable for baking. See photo at right.

Preheat oven to 350 degrees

6 eggs, beaten
1 cup milk
1 cup sugar
1 tsp vanilla
1 tsp cinnamon
5-6 slices of coarse bread, cubed
1/4 cup dark brown sugar

You can add chopped apples, pecans or raisins, optional.

Put a layer of bread cubes on the bottom of each of the ramekins or about 1/2 full. Place a 1/2 teaspoon of brown sugar in the center.

In a large bowl, combine beaten eggs, milk, sugar, vanilla and cinnamon, mix thoroughly. Add chopped apples, pecans or raisins to mixture now, mix well.

Pour mixture equally into the ramekins until full. Sprinkle some cinnamon sugar on top, optional. Bake in oven at 350 degrees for 20 minutes or until done. These will puff up a little and then flatten out some once they are slightly cool. Serve warm with a small pitcher of warm maple syrup. Enjoy !

Hearty Soups

Corn Chowder

This is one of those hearty soups that really hits the spot on a cool and chilly day in the fall. I love serving them in small mini bowls when I'm doing a harvest type tasting buffet. I usually serve 2-3 different soup recipes, so my guests can try different ones. You will need 12 - 15 small ceramic bowls or ramekins, 2-3 oz. See photo at right.

1 pkg of frozen corn, 16 oz, thawed
1 chopped grilled chicken breast, optional
1 red bell pepper, finely chopped
3 cups whole milk
3 tbsp flour
salt and pepper
fresh parsley for garnish, optional

2 potatoes, diced
3 green onions, finely chopped
1 cup chicken broth
2 tbsp butter or margarine
1 egg, beaten

Peel and cut up potatoes into 1/2 cubes and place in a pot of water. Boil until just tender. Drain the water off the potatoes. Leave potatoes in pot, add the corn, green onions and red peppers, the chicken broth, butter and 2-1/2 cups milk. Simmer for about 30 minutes.

In a small jar or lidded container, add the remaining 1/2 cup milk, egg and flour. Shake well. You may need to add a little more milk to make this sauce thinner. Slowly add mixture to soup. Stir constantly until thickened. Add the chopped chicken. Salt and pepper to taste.

Simmer for another 15-20 minutes. Serve in small ceramic ramekins or mini bowls. If you are making this soup for a buffet, I usually pre-heat my mini bowls with boiling water before filling them with the hot soup. This will help keep them hotter longer. This makes more than enough to fill 12-15 mini bowls. Garnish with some fresh parsley. Enjoy !

Country Multi Bean Soup

This is another one of my family favorites. Whenever we have ham for a family dinner or get together, I get the ham bone and always make a large pot of bean soup. Delicious when served with toasted french bread. You will need 12 -15 mini-soup dishes 2-3 oz each for a tasting buffet. See photo at right. This recipe will make more than enough to fill these containers.

one large stock pot, half full of water
ham bone, chunk of ham or several ham hocks
bay leaf
several stalks of celery, cut up
a couple of carrots, sliced
one small onion, cut up

2 large ham slices, cubed
1 can stewed or diced tomatoes
one large jar of Randall's multi-beans, drained
one large jar of Randall's navy beans, drained
1/4 cup instant mashed potatoes

Place the ham bone, bay leaf, celery, carrots and onion with the water in the stock pot and simmer for about 6 hours.

Remove bone and any fat. Add the chunks of ham, tomatoes, all the beans and simmer for another hour or so. Add the instant mashed potatoes and stir thoroughly. This is really good when made the day before and reheated. Serve in little mini soups bowls for a cocktail party, tasting buffet or wide rimmed soup bowls for dinner. Serve with toasted French bread. Pre-heat your bowls with boiling water to keep the soup piping hot. Enjoy !

Chicken Gumbo

This is not quite a traditional New Orleans style soup recipe, but it has all the flavors. You will need 12 -15 mini soup bowls or ramekins for serving, see photo at right.

2 - 3 boneless chicken breasts
2 tbsp cooking oil
8 cups water
3 tomatoes, chopped
1 cup of canned or frozen corn, thawed
1 cup sliced okra or chopped zucchini
1 green pepper, chopped
1/4 cup diced onion
1 chopped carrot
1 stalk of celery, chopped
one slice of cooked bacon, crumbled
dash of cayenne pepper, optional
1 cup of small salad shrimp and or polish sausage, sliced (optional)
salt and pepper
1 cup uncooked rice

Cut chicken into bite size pieces and saute in the bottom of the pot with some cooking oil for about 5 minutes or so or until done. The chicken can brown a little. This will help add a little color to the broth.

Carefully add the water to the pot, then add the rest of the ingredients. Simmer uncovered for about 30 minutes until all the vegetables and rice are tender. Serve hot in the mini soup bowls. Enjoy !

French Onion Soup

This is as traditional as it gets and really delicious. You will need 12 small crock-type ramekins or mini tasting bowls, see photo at right.

3 large onions, thinly sliced
2 tbsp butter or margarine
2 tsp flour
4 cups beef broth
pinch of salt to taste
1/4 cup grated or shredded parmesan, mozzarella or swiss cheese
12 round slices of toasted bread, slightly smaller than the size of your mini soup crocks or handful of toasted croutons.
1/2 cup grated or shredded parmesan cheese

In a large deep skillet, melt butter slowly, saute the onions until they are lightly colored. Stir in the flour and cook until the onions are a darker brown. Do not burn. Add the beef stock and cover the pan and simmer for about 30 minutes.

Ladle the soup into prewarmed mini crocks. Place a piece of toasted bread or croutons on top and pour a little of the broth over them. Sprinkle generously with grated cheese. Place all the filled crocks of soup on a cookie sheet and place under a broiler for a few minutes, until cheese is golden brown. Serve hot, with toasted french bread or any soup cracker. Enjoy !

Ham and Potato Soup

This is another very hearty soup that is great when you have left-over ham. I love serving it at a tasting or cocktail party in mini bowls. It makes a great presentation. You will need 12 -15 mini-soup dishes 2-3 oz each. See photo at right.

6 potatoes, peeled and diced
one bay leaf
several stalks of celery, cut up
a couple of carrots, sliced
one small onion, cut up
2 large ham slices, cut into small cubes
some water

2 cups half & half or whole milk

mini dumplings:
2 eggs, beaten
1/2 cup flour
pinch of salt
milk

To make the mini dumplings, combine the eggs, flour, salt and milk in a bowl. Mix like making a pie crust, but do not mix it too much. Lay the dough on a floured surface and flatten to about an 1/8 of an inch or so. You can use a rolling pin if you want. Take a pizza cutting wheel and slice the dough in long thin strips. Cut these strips into 1" pieces. You are going to be making fat little noodle type dumplings. Let air dry for an hour or so.

In a stock pot, add the first 6 ingredients and cover with water. Simmer for an hour or so or until the potatoes are just tender. Add the cream or milk. Simmer until hot. Add the mini dumplings and simmer for another 30 minutes. This is really good when made the day before and reheated. Serve in little mini soups bowls or crocks for a cocktail party or wide rimmed soup bowls for dinner. Enjoy !

84

Bisques and Cream Soups

Cream of Asparagus Soup

This is an asparagus lovers dream. A rich and creamy soup that is wonderful served at a tasting party but equally as good served before dinner. You will need 12 -15 mini soup bowls or espresso cups for a more unique presentation, see photo at right.

1 lb fresh asparagus, parboiled (or canned asparagus)
1/2 cup pistachios, blanched and mashed
1/2 lb or 2 sticks of butter or margarine
3 tbsp flour
4 cups chicken broth
2 stalks of celery. diced
2 sprigs of fresh basil or 1/4 tsp dried basil
pinch of salt
pinch of cayenne pepper
5 egg yolks
1 tbsp lemon juice

Melt butter in a large saucepan. Add flour to make a roux and whisk in the chicken broth. Add the celery, basil, salt and cayenne pepper. Simmer about 45 minutes.

Parboil the asparagus in a microwavable bowl for just a few minutes to soften. Then add asparagus and mashed pistachios to soup mixture and cook another 15-20 minutes. Working in batches, put several cups of soup at a time in a blender or food processor and puree until smooth.

Return to cleaned pan and reheat slowly. Take a cup or so of soup and beat in the egg yolks. Add this mixture back into the simmering soup. Add the lemon juice and simmer until hot but not boiling. Serve hot. This is especially good served with thin, toasted bread strips. Enjoy !

Butternut Squash Soup

This is one of my favorite soups to make in the fall. It is rich and creamy and I love to serve it in unusual mini containers. The recipe makes 12 or more servings in small deep glass or ceramic bowls, 3-4 oz each. See photo at right.

2 butternut squash, split and seeds removed
3-4 stalks of celery, chopped
1 parsnip, peeled and chopped
4 garlic cloves, chopped
1 cup of heavy cream
2 sprigs of fresh thyme or 1/2 tsp dried thyme
pinch of nutmeg and cayenne pepper

1 large onion, chopped
1 carrot, peeled and chopped
4 fresh mushrooms, chopped
2 cups of chicken broth
2 tbsp butter or margarine
salt and coarse black pepper

Place the squash on a microwavable dish and microwave about 20 minutes or until soft. In a large pot, saute the chopped celery, carrots, parsnip, mushrooms, garlic in the butter until soft. Mash the vegetables. Once the squash is slightly cooled, scoop out the squash and place in the pot with the mashed vegetables. Mix everything together. Add the chicken broth and simmer for about 45 minutes.

If you like a more coarse textured soup, leave it as is. If you want a creamier soup, take an electric mixer and whip until slightly smooth. Add the heavy cream, fresh thyme, nutmeg and cayenne pepper. Mix well. Season with salt and pepper. Serve hot in small mini bowls or espresso cups. Enjoy !

Cream of Potato Soup

I love to make this soup along with the butternut squash and asparagus soups and serve all three in a soup trio (three mini bowls or espresso cups served on a long narrow platter). This makes a great presentation when served before your dinner party.

You will need several little individual ceramic ramekins, espresso cups or small bowls. See photo at right.

1-1/2 lbs potatoes, peeled and chopped
1 carrot, peeled and chopped
2 stalks of celery, chopped
2 cups heavy cream or half and half
salt and pepper

2 tbsp butter or margarine
1 small onion, chopped
3 cups chicken broth
1 bay leaf
pinch of nutmeg

In a large saucepan over medium heat, saute the butter, carrot, onion, celery for about 10 minutes. Add potatoes, bay leaf, chicken broth. Bring just to a boil and simmer for 30 minutes or so, until all vegetables are tender.

Puree the slightly cooled vegetable mixture in a food processor or blender. If you want your soup chunkier, do not process as long. Return to pot, add heavy cream, salt, pepper and nutmeg. Simmer over medium heat until hot, but do not boil. Serve in some wonderful little ceramic bowls or ramekins. Garnish with some croutons. Enjoy !

Cream of Parsnip Soup

Follow the recipe from above, but instead of using potatoes, use parsnips. Prepare the same way and serve. Enjoy !

Seafood Crab Bisque

This seafood bisque reminds me of a small cafe in the seaside town of Ogunquit, Maine. The chunky creamy texture is a delight to your taste buds and makes a delicious appetizer at your next tasting party. I like to use unusual mini containers to make it a more unique presentation. You will need 12 ceramic mini bowls about 3-4 oz each, see photo at right.

2 cans (6oz) of crab meat
1 large onion, chopped
3 carrots, chopped
1 tsp thyme
pinch of cayenne pepper

4 cups chicken broth
2 stalks of celery, chopped
1 bay leaf
1 cup heavy cream
salt

6" chunk of day old French bread, crust removed and finely crumbled

In a microwaveable bowl, place the onion, celery and carrots with about a cup of water. Microwave for about 3 minutes until the vegetables are tender. Save the liquid. Take the vegetables and place in a food processor or hand mash until smooth.

In a large pot, bring chicken broth, crab meat, the vegetable liquid, the vegetable puree, bay leaf, cayenne pepper and thyme to a good simmer. Simmer for about 30 minutes or so. Add the crumbled bread a spoonful at a time until it starts to thicken. Add the heavy cream and simmer another 10 minutes. You may need to add another spoonful of bread crumbs to keep this thick and creamy.

Serve with some homemade toasted bread sticks. Enjoy !

Vegetable Bisque

This vegetable bisque has a lot more unusual and unique flavors than your traditional tomato basil bisque found on page 98. This is perfect with various appetizers served in little mini tasting containers. You will need about 12 mini soup bowls, see photo at right.

1 large (28 oz) can of diced or stewed tomatoes
1 large onion, chopped
3 carrots, chopped
1 green pepper, chopped
1 bay leaf
1 cup heavy cream

2 cups chicken broth
3-4 stalks of celery, chopped
1 zucchini, chopped
2 potatoes, peeled and chopped
1 tsp thyme
pinch of salt and cayenne pepper

small 6" chunk of day old French bread, crust removed and crumbled

In a large microwavable bowl or casserole, place the onion, celery, carrots, zucchini, green pepper and potatoes with about 2 cups water. Microwave for about 10 minutes until the vegetables are tender. Save the liquid. Take the vegetables and place in a food processor or hand mash until smooth.

In a stockpot, bring chicken broth, the vegetable liquid, the vegetable puree, bay leaf, cayenne pepper and thyme to a good simmer. Simmer for about 30 minutes or so. Add the crumbled bread crumbs, a little at a time, until the soup starts to thicken. Add the heavy cream and simmer another 10 minutes. Serve with some homemade toast sticks or some long crackers as in the photo. Serve and Enjoy !

Tomato Basil Bisque

A traditional tomato soup that is healthy, yet rich in flavor. I love this soup when served with small mini-grilled cheese sandwiches. You will need 12-15 small ramekins or small ceramic shooters, see photo at right.

1 large can (28oz) of diced or stewed tomatoes
few tablespoons of chopped fresh basil
1 small onion, sliced
1 bay leaf
1 tsp sugar
1 tsp salt
1/4 tsp pepper
1 cup heavy cream or whole milk
1/4 cup sour cream for garnish or croutons

Heavy cream will make this soup creamy and delicious, but not as healthy as if you were to use whole or 2% milk.

In a food processor or blender, puree the tomatoes and onion. I will sometimes just use an electric mixer right in my soup pan. Place mixture in a large saucepan. Add the fresh basil, sugar, salt and pepper. Simmer for 10 minutes.

Stir in heavy cream and simmer another 10 -15 minutes until hot, but do not boil. Serve in the little ceramic shooters or ramekins. Drizzle a little sour cream on top or add a handful of croutons. Serve and Enjoy !

Cold or Chilled Soups

Gazpacho Soup

This is a great cold soup for a summer get together with family and friends. It's cold and refreshing and really festive when served in tall glass shooters or any unusual glass mini container. You will need 12 -15 mini containers. See photo at right.

3 bell peppers, 1 green, 1 red, 1 yellow, cored and chopped
1 zucchini, sliced   1 onion, sliced
4 ripe tomatoes or one can of diced tomatoes   1 cucumber, sliced
1 cup tomato juice   1 cup of fresh or frozen corn
1/2 tsp crushed pepper   1 tbsp lemon juice
1 garlic clove   2 tbsp chopped cilantro
1/2 tsp cumin   1 tsp salt and pepper
1 cucumber for garnish or several celery sticks

You will need a large storage container, suitable for storing the soup in the refrigerator.

Using a food processor or a blender, finely chop or puree all the ingredients. Work in batches, taking a few slices of each vegetable and pureeing them together. Put the pureed mixture in the storage container and proceed on to the second batch and so on.

If you like a smoother gazpacho, puree each batch a little longer. Stir in the remaining spices. Refrigerate a few hours until cold. For a garnish, take the remaining cucumber and cut into 3" chunks, then cut these pieces into 1/4" strips. Use these as a kind of stir stick in a tall glass soup shooter. Serve and Enjoy !

Avocado Mint Soup

This is like eating guacamole through a straw. Creamy, minty and refreshingly cool. Great for a summer brunch and especially festive when served in a unusual mini tasting bowl. You will need 12 - 15 of these mini glass soup bowls, see photo at right.

2 avocados, peeled and pitted
1/4 cup lemon or lime juice
1/4 cup fresh parsley or cilantro, chopped
2 cups chicken broth
1 cup heavy cream
1/2 tsp chili powder
salt and freshly ground pepper
2 tbsp. finely chopped fresh mint
1 cup fresh diced tomatoes, for garnish
handful of tostada chips for garnish

Cut the avocado into chunks and place in a bowl with the lemon juice. Mash with a fork leaving it kind of lumpy. Season with salt and pepper. Place the avocado mixture in a soup pan and slowly add the chicken broth. Stir and simmer on low heat.

Slowly add the cream and freshly chopped parsley, mint, chili powder, mix well. Bring the soup just to a boil and simmer a few minutes.

This can be served hot or cold. Serve hot in mini ramekins or cold in small glass bowls. Garnish with a few pieces of fresh diced tomato on top. Serve with a few tostada chips on the side. Enjoy !

Cucumber Yogurt Soup

This is a very light and refreshing summer soup and extemely healthy. I sometimes serve this along with the gazpacho soup on page 102 to have a delicious variety at a tasting party. They are a real compliment to one another. You will need 12 small glass bowls or shooters, about 4 oz each. See photo at right.

2 medium cucumbers, remove seeds and chop
2 green onions, chopped
1 tsp salt
1/4 tsp dill weed
1 tsp fresh mint, finely chopped (optional)
1/4 cup fresh parsley
1/4 tsp olive oil
1/4 tsp vinegar
2 cups plain yogurt

1 cucumber cut in half and then cut into thin strips, for garnish.

Place the first six ingredients in a food processor or blender and puree until smooth. Add the oil, vinegar, yogurt and blend until mixed well. Chill in a storage container for 3-4 hours. Serve in small shooter glasses with a cucumber stick for garnish. Enjoy !

Mini Salads

Cranberry Cocktail Salad

This is one of my favorite little mini tasters. I will use it often as a salad as much as I would for a dessert. It is tangy and zesty and is a great compliment to any poultry appetizer. I like to serve it in shot glasses or mini dessert dishes. You will need 12 small glass dishes, 2-3 oz. each. See photo at right.

1 cup fresh cranberries, finely ground or chopped
1 apple, cored and finely chopped
1 small can crushed pineapple, drained
1/2 cup sugar
1/2 orange, finely chopped with rind and juice
1/2 cup chopped celery
1/2 cup chopped pecans
2 -3 oz box red gelatin
2 cups hot water to dissolve gelatin & 1 cup cold water
several orange slices or whipped topping for garnish

In a large glass mixing bowl, add red gelatin and 2 cups boiling water, stir until completely dissolved. Add one cup cold water and stir. Place in refrigerator to set while you are chopping up remaining ingredients.

Combine all chopped ingredients in another large mixing bowl, stir in sugar until dissolved slightly. You can use food processor to chop everything finely. Pour partially set gelatin into the the bowl of chopped ingredients and blend thoroughly.

Once everything is mixed up, spoon into any small glass container and refrigerate until set, 2-3 hours or overnight. Garnish with a slice of fresh orange or a dollop of whipped topping. Enjoy !

Shepherd's Salad (Turkish Tabouli)

I borrowed this wonderful little salad from our friends in the Middle East. A small mini portion is just enough because of its zesty combination of parsley and spices. I will often serve it in these shot glasses for a more unique presentation. You will need 12 shot glasses or small glass bowls, 3 oz each. See photo at right.

4 fresh ripe tomatoes, finely chopped
1 cucumber, seeds removed and finely chopped
1 large onion, finely chopped
1/2 cup fresh parsley, chopped
1/2 cup fresh cilantro, chopped
2 tbsp olive oil
coarse ground pepper
salt

In a large mixing bowl, combine tomatoes, cucumber and onion. Add parsley and cilantro. Mix together with the olive oil. Salt and pepper to taste. Refrigerate for an hour or so. Serve in small shot glasses or mini bowls. Enjoy !

Caprese Salad (tomato, mozzarella, basil)

This is another one of my favorite tasting salads. It is easy to prepare anytime of the year, because cherry tomatoes are always available. But the traditional version uses fresh, vine ripened tomatoes in the peak of summer. Nothing is more delicious. Making it in mini tasting dishes just adds to the fantastic presentation. I often use Italian or balsamic dressing when I'm in a hurry. You will need 12 glass bowls or mini dishes. See photo on the right.

24 cherry tomatoes, halved
1 small can sliced black olives
1 lb fresh buffalo mozzarella, diced
1/2 cup fresh basil, chopped or torn into small pieces
1/4 cup olive oil
2 tbsp balsamic vinegar
salt and coarse fresh black pepper

You can also add 1/2 cup finely chopped sweet onions or green onions.

In a mixing bowl combine the first four ingredients. Toss with the olive oil and balsamic vinegar. Season to taste with the salt and pepper. Serve in small glass containers on a long ceramic tray. Enjoy !

Garden Gelatin Salad

This is a wonderful gelatin salad that can be adapted to almost any flavor of gelatin. I regularly use lime, but you can use either lemon or orange. You can also add almost any type of chopped up fresh vegetable or fruit. I like to use the mini parfait glasses or shooters; they really add a unique twist to this presentation. You will need 12 or so of the small shooter parfait glasses, see photo at right.

1 box (6 oz) of lime gelatin
2 cup boiling water
1 cup cold water
1 carrot, finely chopped
1 green pepper, finely chopped
1 red pepper, finely chopped
1 small can of diced pineapple, drained
1 stalk of celery, finely chopped

In a microwavable bowl, add 2 cups of water and microwave to a boil. Add lime gelatin and stir until dissolved, about 2 minutes. Add 1 cup very cold water or a cup of crushed ice. Stir a few minutes or until the ice is dissolved. Crushed ice will partially help set up the gelatin in a few minutes.

In a large mixing bowl, combine all remaining ingredients. Mix well.

In the shooter glasses, fill about half full with finely chopped veggie mixture. Then cover with lime gelatin. Tap the glass softly on a surface so the gelatin settles and covers the veggies. Add some more veggie mixture and fill almost to the top with lime gelatin. Tap again. Sprinkle a few veggie pieces on top for garnish. Refrigerate for a couple of hours to set. Serve and Enjoy !

Honey Fruit Salad

This is another one of those quick and simple recipes that just bursts with flavor. The combination of basil and mint adds a unique twist to an everyday fruit salad. I like to make a bowl of it and serve it in little tasting bowls. This recipe fills 12 or so small tasting bowls, 4 oz. each, see photo to the right.

2 cups diced fresh pineapple or canned pineapple tidbits
1 cup diced honeydew or cantaloupe melon
1 cup diced mango
1/4 cup finely chopped red bell pepper
2 tbsp diced fresh basil
1 tbsp diced fresh mint
1 tbsp lime juice
4 tbsp honey
1/4 tsp ginger

Mix all ingredients in a large mixing bowl. Let stand 10 -15 minutes to blend. Divide mixture equally in the 12 small tasting dishes as shown at right. Serve and Enjoy !

Cucumber Gelatin Salad

This is a very refreshing summer salad, but it is also great any time of the year. It is pretty easy to make and very tasty and refreshing. I like to serve it in little glass mini bowls. You will need 12 or so of these small glass bowls, see photo at right.

1 box (6 oz) of lime or lemon gelatin
2 cups boiling water
1 cup cold water
1 pkg (3 oz) cream cheese, softened
1 cup mayonnaise or sour cream
1/4 cup green onions, finely chopped
1 cucumber, seeded and finely chopped
1 tbsp lemon juice
dash of salt

1/2 cup sour cream
1 tbsp sugar

In a microwavable bowl, add 2 cups water and microwave to a boil. Add lime or lemon gelatin and stir until dissolved, about 2 minutes. Stir in 1 cup cold water. Add the cream cheese, mayonnaise, salt and lemon juice. Beat smooth with an electric mixer. Chill until partially set. Stir in cucumber and green onions.

Fill the small glass dishes or shooter glasses with gelatin mixture. Refrigerate for a couple of hours to completely set. Mix the remaining sour cream and the sugar, add a spoonful of mixture to the top of each bowl. Serve and Enjoy !

Tomato Basil Couscous Salad

A very light and refreshing salad that has a little hint of the Moroccan cuisine. It looks great when served in these little mini tasting dishes. You will need 12 or so of these small glass dishes, see photo at right.

4 fresh ripe tomatoes, diced
1 cup cilantro or parsley, finely chopped
2 tbsp olive oil
1 tbsp vinegar
1 cucumber, seeded and diced
1 onion, finely chopped
1 lb couscous
1 tbsp fresh lemon juice
fresh ground pepper and pinch of salt

Combine the diced tomatoes, cucumbers, cilantro, onions and couscous in a large mixing bowl. Toss with the fresh lemon juice.

In another smaller mixing bowl, combine the vinegar and olive oil with some fresh ground pepper and a pinch of salt, whisk until well blended.

Combine the vinaigrette with the tomato mixture until well blended.

Fill the small glass dishes with the salad, place on a large platter and serve. Enjoy !

INDEX

APPETIZERS

Bacon Spread	30
Beef and Pickle Roll Ups	20
Cucumber Tea Sandwiches	38
Cheese Cubes	52
Chicken Teriyaki Kabobs	54
Deviled Egg Spread	32
Egg Souffle	70
Festive Olive Kabobs	28
Feta Cheese Toast	24
French Toast Souffle	72
Guacamole Roll Ups	46
Ham & Pineapple Skewers	34
Hawaiian Sweet & Sour Meatballs	58
Italian Bruschetta	18
Italian Bruschetta with Cheese	18
Jambalaya Kabobs	62
Mango Salsa with Shrimp	42
Mango Salsa with Chicken	42
Meatballs with Spicy Sauce	66
Mini Crab Cakes	60
MozzarellaTomato & Basil Caprese	26
Prosciutto and Melon	22
Pizza Mediterranean	64
Roasted Vegetable Tarts	56
Salami and Cheese Roll Ups	20
Simply Chutney	36
Stuffed Mushrooms	50
Sushi Teriyaki Clouds	44
Texas Party Quiches	68

SALADS

Caprese Salad	114
Cranberry Cocktail Salad	110
Cucumber Gelatin Salad	120
Garden Gelatin Salad	116
Honey Fruit Salad	118
Shepherd's Salad	112
Tomato Basil Couscous Salad	122

SOUPS

Asparagus, Cream of	88
Avocado Mint Soup	104
Butternut Squash Soup	90
Chicken Gumbo	80
Corn Chowder	76
Country Multi Bean Soup	78
Cucumber Yogurt Soup	106
French Onion Soup	82
Gazpacho Soup	102
Ham & Potato Soup	84
Potato, Cream of	92
Parsnip, Cream of	92
Seafood Crab Bisque	94
Tomato Basil Bisque	98
Vegetable Bisque	96

About the author.

Robert Zollweg is a native of Toledo, Ohio and has been in the tabletop industry for almost 40 years. He designs glassware, flatware and ceramic products for the retail and foodservice industry. He has worked with all of the major retailers including Crate and Barrel, Williams-Sonoma, Macy's, Pier One Imports, Cost Plus World Market, Bed Bath & Beyond, JCPenneys, Target, Walmart and Sears, to name a few. Most of his professional career has been with Libbey Glass in Toledo, Ohio. He has traveled the world extensively looking for color and design trends and the right products to design and bring to the retail and foodservice marketplace. Robert has always had a passion for entertaining. His first cookbook was on mini desserts, so "Just Tasting" with these mini appetizers, soups and salads will continue this passion. He is also an artist-painter and works primarily with acrylic on canvas using bold colors. His painting style has been called by many as abstract expressionism. He currently lives in his home in Toledo's Historic Old West End and in the artistic community of Saugatuck, Michigan.

To find more information about Robert Zollweg, visit his web site at www.zollwegart.com

I hope you have enjoyed my cookbook on "Just Tasting", using mini appetizers, soups and salads. It should help to make your next casual get together a little easier and a lot more fun and delicious.

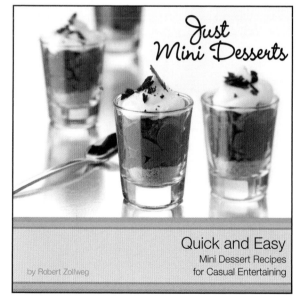

My cookbook on quick and easy mini desserts, a wonderful compliment to "Just Tasting" is also available at area retailers or at www.zollwegart.com

Enjoy, Robert